# *Transformations*

First published 2023 by The Hedgehog Poetry Press

Published in the UK by
The Hedgehog Poetry Press
Coppack House, 5
Churchill Avenue
Clevedon
BS21 6QW

www.hedgehogpress.co.uk

ISBN: 978-1-916830-00-4

9 8 7 6 5 4 3 2 1

A CIP Catalogue record for this book is available from the British Library.

# Transformations

*Poems inspired by the work of Elisabeth Frink*

## Beth Brooke

*With grateful thanks to the family of Elisabeth Frink and to the Dorset Museum for their help and encouragement and for permission to use the image of the* Green Man

# Contents

# HARBINGER BIRDS

Beaks, claws, wings,
we foreshadow,
invade your dark places.

Beaks, claws, wings,
we are shrapnel
ripping through grey sky.

We are disquiet,
our song splinters silence,
we are predator and prey,

in the glint of our eyes
your own fragility.

# GOURMAND

*bronze 1952*

The raven thinks about flesh,

remembers the bright reds
of battlefield gashes.

Its claws flex, as it contemplates
tearing the fat and muscle from the
newly dead,

its beak imagines bloodied gobbets
of the khaki-clad and of lonely woodland suicides.

It will graze the gamekeeper's gibbet:
its scraps are tenderised by time,
maggoty, they melt upon the tongue,

but what it prizes more than anything
is the chance to grip the breast
as the pulse flutters, then peck and peck

until it finds the beating heart beneath the skin.

# MAN AND BIRD

*ink on paper, 1953, Dorset Museum*

*Speak to me,* says the crow,
*give me your story.*
*Tell me the roots and branches*
*of where you chose to roost*
*and build your nest.*

The man settles the crow upon his chest,
the needle prick of its claws
a small discomfort
in exchange for company,
for the richness of the crow's attention.

*I come,* he says, *from the scent of the sea.*
*I was seeded by the ocean*
*in the valleys between chalk hills.*

*In autumn the hawthorns*
*of the inland slopes*
*are bent by salt breezes*
*and heavy with berries,*
*crimson, tough-skinned*
*against the blasts of winter.*
*They were my roost.*

*I will go there,* says the crow,
*I will gather berries for you.*
*The scent of the sea will be on them.*
*It will comfort you.*

# THE UNKNOWN POLITICAL PRISONER REFLECTS

*Tribute Head II, bronze, 1977 Dorset Museum*

I live too much inside my own head;
it is the only place left to me
where the dark is kind and
not an instrument of torture.

In my head is a whole world:
the way it feels
to hold an infant as she sleeps,
head nestled in the hollow of my neck,

the memory of a lover's mouth on mine,
hungry yet restrained,
grazing on the meadow of my skin.

Today I sit in the square of sunlight,
note its warmth, even on this winter morning,
the glass and the walls keep out the wind.

I imagine the sound of a stream,
think I am home again,
the whole day ahead of me.

I pretend sleep between linen sheets,
pretend permission          to sing
          or not to sing
without fear of consequence.

# INTERNAL MONOLOGUE OF THE WILD BOAR

*bronze 1969, Dorset Museum*

The light is  dense
soon it will fall from
the tree  ripe
dark as acorns
the         earth
is full of movement
            worms
leatherjackets
squirm in the mouth,
wriggle
            down the gullet
the scent of fungus
leaves
            breast of a crow
a garnish of beetle
crab apples
gullet      ripe
fungus
            crow

the earth is full

# DOG

*bronze 1958, Dorset Museum*

stands on spindle legs,
raises his head, ears slicked back
against his skull,

howls with joy
at the rush of breeze, at
the thousand messages
it carries for him alone.

Nose points the way,
tugs at the leash,
waits, eager for the man
to catch up.

# MAN AND BABOON

*gouache and ink, 1987, Dorset Museum*

*Sit*, the baboon indicates,
*here*;
it taps the ground
then turns its head
away.

The man sits,
raw-skinned,
muscle and feeling exposed to view,

makes fists of his hands,
to serve in place of words;
the words he does have
are spat from the mouth
like loose teeth after a beating.

*Look*, says the baboon,
*the forest is burning.*

# BABOON

*bronze 1989, Dorset Museum*

Aren't we brothers under the skin,
my thumbs as able to oppose
as yours,
as likely to rip the tenderness
from fear, explore its raw edges?
Don't we both make fists of ourselves?


And after, when we wrap our arms
around one another to comfort
our regret,
do we not watch the same sun
bleach the morning yellow?

# CHINESE HORSE I  (ROLLING HORSE)

*bronze 1989, Dorset Museum*

I am body
machine
heart engine  blood
muscle   bone


I am
breath
snort      neigh
           moist warmth
condensed cloudlets of
in and out
heavy with running

sound

vibration of hooves on ground
thunder of scattered gravel

I am
exultation
rolling    rolling
in fields
the utter feel of it
           the scent and rub of earth

# AN INTERVIEW WITH THE HORSEMEN OF THE APOCALYPSE ON THE EVE OF THEIR RETROSPECTIVE EXHIBITION

*Three Riders, lithograph, 1974 by Elisabeth Frink, Dorset Museum*

This lithograph is from the Seventies,
Pestilence wasn't so active then.
There was talk of him leaving, but
as you know he's upped his game since:
AIDS, SARS, Ebola, that kind of thing
and with this latest, he's surpassed himself.

Famine? That aspect of the work
is very strong; it was a good decision
to diversify into climate futures -
mostly flood and drought,
deforestation; the initial data
looks quite promising.

Modernisation is key and
War has made good use
of new technologies,
cyber, digital;
it's a growth industry,
less face-to-face,
more drone, remote control.
We have an
R&D department now,
it's great to feel that we
can influence
the direction of travel.

Death obviously remains the CEO,
his finger on the pulse -
on all the pulses actually.
  *(laughs).*

That said, he's expanded operations
in association with the climate brief,
we're looking at non-human populations
- mass extinctions right across the globe.

You have to beware of entropy,
keep moving forward - that's what we do.

# HORSES AT THE BATTLE OF PHILIPPI

*book illustration, Horace: The Odes, 1987*

The steam and stink of fear is all encompassing;
riderless horses, flanks slippery with sweat

plunge through the chaos, their eyes made wild,
made mad by the thrust and noise of war.

They run, slip on earth made wet by the blood
and piss and excrement of man and animal.

One horse stumbles, hooves flail against air,
the crash of its landing splinters the thigh

of the man on its back who had thought himself
warrior, strong, redoubtable.

And the screams of both are high-pitched,
terrible.

# THE BIRDMAN AT MANCHESTER AIRPORT
# MAKES HIS CONFESSION

*1962*

We are envious, full of longing,
incapable of looking
at the setting of a raspberry-peach sun
without desire.
We want to hurl ourselves
into its horizon, possess
the sunrise, the sunset,
the light and the dark,
offered freely
to every living thing.
We watch hawks, held
in the cupped hands of the warm air
and cannot help but strap our arms
to crudely fashioned wings,
lunge at the heavens,
bold as Icarus.

# FALLING MAN

*bronze, 1961, Dorset Museum*

In my dreams I watch them plummet,
spew smoke in spiral streamers
through the sky.

I do not want to look;
I cannot help myself.

In the morning we race over
scorched ground. Scavengers,
we pick over the choicest morsels.

Later, much later, my dreams
turn the machines to men.
I watch them fall,

spindle arms flung forward
they dive through a waterless sea
and the earth reaches out to receive them.

I never want to look;
I cannot stop myself.

# MARCHING SONG OF THE DICTATORS

*Goggle Head, bronze, 1969*

We swagger
      know where the bodies
are buried

      don't make us mad

avert your gaze when we visit your home
      take your sister     shoot your brother

we are    Vladimir Saddam       Radovan
and there are others

kings of the world

      we know how to make you disappear
from a public place

      can tenderise muscle without so much
as raising a gloved fist

we can strip you of everything     everything
we feel your fear
we hide our eyes from you
you cannot see us

# THE RIACE WARRIORS

*bronze, 1986*

We hold fear in our open palms,
close fists around it
ready
        to fling ourselves
        into the smoke
splinters
and choking dust

it settles  on our faces
makes
        ghosts of us
renders us blind
invisible

when we emerge from the darkness
into the settling light
we will
        be ready
to fight
a cobweb touch of terror
        on our forearms
the rapid beating  of our hearts
we are what the world looks like
        after the bombs have fallen

# THE ANGUISH OF THE HIRELING THUG

*Soldier's Head II, bronze 1965, Dorset Museum*

I fight. I have been trained; there is a skill needed for the breaking of bones and the disfigurement of flesh. You have to be taught where to insert the blade and I am good at it. I am only the instrument, not the thought behind the thrust. I am your hireling thug: point me in the direction you want me to go.

Sometimes in the night
I dream of blood and screaming
my heart fists me


My jaw is heavy, neck thickset. I am machine, gun, grenade. Call me cannon firer, cannon fodder, wham bam, job done. Take the dosh at the end of the month; piss it up with the lads.

A broken mirror
reflects in fractured image
the anguish inside

# JUDAS SPEAKS (WITH ACCOMPANYING MARGINALIA)

*bronze, 1963*

There is a robin (1) in the tree,
its scolding chit chit call
is like a needle prick upon the skin.
It only speaks to me.

You could speak to me,
could listen as I shed myself.
No,
do not say that Satan entered me, (2)
grant me at least the dignity
of my actions being my own. (3)

Could you please stand further off?
I cannot see you, but I feel your shadow,
intimidating. I sense
your expression, know your disgust (4)

yet what I have done is set
to change the world.
You shouldn't judge me;
I am perfectly capable of doing that
myself.

# THE MARGINALIA

*(1)*

*Robins are linked
to crucifixion mythologies.
It's said one tried to pluck
the thorns from the Messiah's
head, a drop of His blood creating
that iconic red breast.*

*(2)*

*John thirteen, verse twenty-seven says
that Satan entered Judas when
he dipped his bread in Christ's dish.
Christ stated that the one who did
would serve Him up to His destruction,
told Judas to be quick.
The question here is, who was
in control?*

*(3)*

*There's been some discourse
as to motivations. Judas never
seems to have articulated
what his motivations might
have been.*

*(4)*

*If one accepts the notion
of free will, his actions
must be viewed as a
betrayal, the disgust inferred,
his own.*

# GREEN MAN

*ink and charcoal on paper,1991, Dorset Museum*

*O Lord, open thou our lips:*
*and our mouth shall shew forth thy praise.*
*(The Book of Common Prayer)*

Praise climbs out of my mouth,
clings to my cheeks like ivy
on the wall of a garden,
searches for the wildness and
wildernesses in which to grow.

The leaves unfurl and soon
there will be a blossoming;
bees will come, sip the sweetness
in my eyes and vibrate their wings
in a hymn to abundance.

My limbs will become branches
where birds will roost, make
chicks of eggs, sing all the while
as though the world depended on it
and we were equal voices in its song.

# THE TRANSFORMATION OF TURMOIL

Iron splinters
fell, like heavy rain
after a sodden summer.

Towns and cities
drowned in rubble.
It cost so very much
to keep wading through;
sometimes we thought
we wouldn't reach the other side.

We walked where
ragged sticks of men regarded us.
Some had eaten their own hearts
to stay alive;
we had no words to comfort them.

Twice, we saw death,
like a poisonous mushroom
toss out its spores.
However high we built our walls,
fear drifted over them.
Like thistledown,
it settled everywhere.

Some of us did the only thing
we knew to do:
we turned the soil,
pulled out the poison roots,
saw what would grow, planted,
learned to think of it
as beautiful.

## ACKNOWLEDGEMENTS

Some of the poems featured in *Transformations* have previously been published, as below:

*Man and Bird* (iambapoet.com Wave 8 2021)

*The Birdman At Manchester Airport Makes His Confession* (Ink Sweat & Tears February 2022)

*Horses At The Battle Of Philippi* (Flight Of The Dragonfly e-journal issue 8 2023)

*Baboon.* (Sarasvati journal 2023 issue 069)